The

Personal

Vocation

Herbert Alphonso, S.J.

THE
PERSONAL   VOCATION

TRANSFORMATION IN DEPTH
THROUGH THE SPIRITUAL EXERCISES

Eighth Edition

Editrice Pontificia Università Gregoriana
Rome, 2002

Cum Permissu Superiorum

ISBN 88-7652-925-X

The illustrations in the book are taken from a selection of graphics drawn by Maria Christa Honekamp FC. The permission of the artist is gratefully acknowledged.

Translated into French, German, Italian, Japanese, Korean, Polish, Portuguese, Slovakian, Slovenian and Spanish.

IN GRATEFUL MEMORY
OF
MY PARENTS GASPAR AND ANNIE
TO WHOM I OWE THE LIVELINESS OF MY FAITH

AND ESPECIALLY
OF
MY SISTER ROSIE
TO WHOM, UNDER GOD,
MORE THAN TO ANYONE ELSE,
I OWE MY BEING TODAY A JESUIT PRIEST

CONTENTS

FOREWORD
TO THE FIRST EDITION

For a long time, indeed for years, several close friends, who have resonated deeply and enthusiastically with what I say about the "Personal Vocation", have been urging me to put down in writing what I have been sharing literally around the world on this topic. In response to these gentle pressures I dealt with the theme of "Personal Vocation" in a series of six cassette-tapes, which our Ignatian Spirituality Centre (CIS) published in 1986 on the theme of "The Contemplative Dimension of Apostolic Religious Life".

But I still had not got down to writing anything on the subject. Early in 1989 I was approached to read a paper at the International Symposium on Psychology and the Spiritual Exercises of St. Ignatius to be held in Salamanca, Spain in September (12-16), 1989 on the theme "La Transformación del Yo en la Experiencia de los Ejercicios Espirituales" (The Transformation of the 'Self' in the Experience of the Spiritual Exercises). Unfortunately I was already committed to some programmes in India scheduled for September 1989, so I begged to be excused from participating in the Salamanca Symposium. While this was accepted, I was urged to send in a written contribution to the Symposium at least for the publication, which would collate into one single volume the principal contributions prepared for the Symposium. It was insistently suggested that I write on the topic of the "Personal Vocation".

And so in early September I dispatched my written contribution on "The Personal Vocation: Transformation in Depth through the Spiritual Exercises". Since this will appear in Spanish in the above-mentioned volume slated to be published during the Ignatian Year (September 1990 - July 1991), I am glad to offer a slightly enlarged English version of it in this booklet form as my humble contribution in preparation for the Ignatian Anniversaries of 1990 and 1991.

What I owe to "my beloved father St. Ignatius" will, I hope, transpire from every page of this little booklet.

Herbert Alphonso, S J.

27th. September, 1989

449th. Anniversary
of the Birth of the Society of Jesus

INTRODUCTION

For several years I had been taught, and had come to believe, that the personal transformation wrought by the Spiritual Exercises of St. Ignatius consisted, through a dynamic process of growing inner freedom, in the "Election", understood either as the discernment of the state of life to which one is called by God or as the reform to be effected, within an already chosen state of life, in areas which would be discerned in the course of the experience of the Exercises. In the latter case, such an "Election" would entail a certain number of definite "resolutions" which, if put into practice, would obtain the desired reform and personal transformation.

Then in 1965 I had such an overpowering experience of the Spirit during my annual eight-day retreat, which worked a complete overhauling and transformation in my personal life and ministry, that I have continued to live of this single greatest grace of my life, and to draw out unceasingly the rich strands of that grace for the true understanding, practice and direction of the Spiritual Exercises of St. Ignatius. A seminal gift and grace, I like to call it in fact, as I am still drawing on it for ever fresh and new vistas that open out for me in the field of all theology and all spirituality, and in my ministry of the Spirit. The central nucleus of a rich personal synthesis for life and ministry is what it has come to be.

What I have characterised above as the single greatest grace of my life is that in that 1965 retreat I discerned my truest and deepest "self", the unrepeatable uniqueness God has given to me in "calling me by name". And I have come to realise that the discernment of that truest and deepest "self" is the authentic, the most profound and radical meaning of the "Election" which is the goal of the Ignatian Exercises. This truest and deepest "self", this God-given uniqueness, I call the "Personal Vocation". Besides, my own personal experience and my ministry of the Spirit have taught me that the deepest transformation in any person's life takes place in the actual living out of this very "Personal Vocation".

I

THE "ELECTION"
OF THE IGNATIAN EXERCISES

It has been said, and written too, that the Spiritual Exercises of St. Ignatius, if not directed to the discernment of one's "state of life", must issue concretely in a certain number of "resolutions", which specifically express the ongoing reform and transformation that must be wrought within one's current personal life-situation. We were all taught, and insistently so, that if such a transformation is really to be effective, these "resolutions" had better be few, very concrete, possible to keep, etc.

Now, quite frankly, what are these so-called "resolutions"? They are decisions which I take to make a determinated, sustained effort about certain points which I have perceived in the course of personal prayer and reflection to be either faulty or deficient on the one hand, or to need positive buttressing and support on the other. For example, such "resolutions" may concern one's relationships with others, or one's task, mission and ministry, or again the self discipline required for a life of prayer or of study, etc. Let us honestly face it: does the taking of these "resolutions" require the whole profound dynamics of the Ignatian Exercises - that is, a sustained praying experience (four to five hours each day for thirty days) leading to a discerning experience under regular and competent spiritual guidance (a review of prayer after each hour of prayer, then taking this experience to a director so that he/she may help the retreatant understand the experience, then accept it and gradually find what God is saying through that experience)? Frankly, the whole thing is entirely out of proportion; as the poet Horace would say: "parturiunt montes, nascetur ridiculus mus" (the mountains are in birth-pangs; what is born is a ridiculous little mouse!). Isn't it true that half-a-day or a day of recollection, which includes prayer, reflection and may-be some consultation, would suffice for the taking of these "resolutions"?

The only thing that would be proportionate to the deep and demanding dynamics of the Exercises would be the taking hold of one's whole and entire life - the totality of it - to turn it over to God. This is what a "conversion" is in its profound biblical sense - a "metanoia", a change of direction. No wonder St. Ignatius spells out the nature and purpose of his Exercises as "every way of preparing and disposing the soul to rid itself of all inordinate attachments and, after their removal, of *seeking and finding the will of God in the disposition of my life for the salvation of my soul*" (*Sp. Exs.* 1). In other words, the goal of the Exercises is "Election", or the seeking and finding of God's will in *the arrangement or ordering or orientation of my life* (= *la disposición de mi vida*) for salvation.

Now one way in which I can understand "God's will in the arrangement or ordering or orientation of my life for salvation" is certainly the state of life to which I am called by God. But it is by no means the only, or even the deepest and most radical, understanding of it: in fact, at its deepest level, "God's will in the arrangement or ordering or orientation of my life for salvation" is my unrepeatable uniqueness, the "name" by which God calls me - that is, my truest or deepest "self", my "Personal Vocation", as I have termed it. For the authentic meaning of "Election" in the process and dynamics of the Ignatian Exercises is a *becoming aware in growing inner freedom of God's personal design or plan for me,* so that I can accept it profoundly in my life to live it out faithfully and generously. And what, I ask, is most radically - even more radically than my "state of life" - God's personal plan and design for me if not my God-given uniqueness, my deepest and truest "self", my "Personal Vocation"?

II

THE PERSONAL VOCATION

A fundamental theme that runs through the Bible is "called by name". This is not the place to marshal the many and rich biblical texts that bear abundant witness to this theme. What it amounts to is: I am not one in a crowd for God, I am not a serialised number nor a catalogued card; I am unrepeatably unique, for God "calls me by name". This reality I may certainly characterise as my "personal identity", or my "personal orientation in life", or my most profound and true "self'. Biblically, however, I prefer to call it my "personal vocation". It is sad that we have often restricted the term "vocation" to priestly and religious "vocations"; grudgingly, perhaps, we are speaking increasingly of the married and lay "vocation". Actually in the Bible the word of God terms every call from God to a specific orientation or mission in life a "vocation".

Perhaps I can best illustrate the meaning of "Personal Vocation" by recounting one from among many actual and similar incidents in my own experience.

Several years ago a middle-aged Jesuit, who has since passed away, came to see me. He was a good friend, so he started to speak spontaneously about his personal life. He shared with me that he had not been praying for many years: even if he did go to prayer - very rarely, he said - he actually did not pray; he was present only bodily, materially. As he spoke of his great negligence in prayer, I got the feeling that he was sort of "hung up" on his negligence in prayer. So I sensed that if I had to be of help to him, I had first to make him take his distance from this "negligence in prayer" with which he was somewhat obsessed, to look at it in perspective. So, very casually, I said to him: "You haven't been praying for a long, long time. Tell me: have you at any time in your life felt *spontaneously* close to God - not because you went through a reasoned process, but *spontaneously,* have you ever felt your heart uplifted and yourself in touch with God, in union with

God?" I had hardly framed the question when he said: "Of course, whenever I look back at my past life and see *how good God has heen to me,* I feel immediately close to God, in touch with God, united with Him". Seeing that he had come alive, that he was talking with deep feeling, a gleam in his eyes, I broke in: "The goodness of God seems to mean a lot to you, the way you are speaking; have you never prayed on the goodness of God?" "Never", he returned, and, taken aback by my question, he got on the defensive and spouted out aggressively: "Besides, how long do you think I can pray on the goodness of God?" - giving me to understand that he would get tired of it. I had listened very carefully to him, so I came in very quietly with: "You just told me you've never tried it; how about trying it before making a judgment that you'll get tired of it?" "Fair enough", he said, and with that he left my room.

Some three weeks later he stormed into my room, gushing forth his great discovery: "You know, Herbie, I can pray always on the goodness of God, pray always on the goodness of God". I must make an open confession: I suppose I had been somewhat bugged by his aggressive defensiveness three weeks earlier, so I very cynically said: "Well, it's only three weeks; perhaps if you tried a little longer, you might get tired of it!" Very visibly before me this Jesuit, who had so enthusiastically been gushing forth his discovery that he could pray always on the goodness of God, became suddenly deflated and slunk out of my room. In a trice I woke up to what had happened and exclaimed to myself: "O my God, I have lost him because of my smart cynicism!" But if I was not good that day, God is good.

Against all my expectations this middle-aged Jesuit did come back to me - not three weeks later, but full four-and-a-half months later. This time he did not storm into my room: he almost tip-toed into it and said emphatically in a quiet whisper: "But really, Herbie, I can pray *always* on the goodness of God". By now I had hopefully learned my lesson, so at once I invited him: "Sit you down, please, Father". And he began to share in touching depth all that the goodness of God had come to mean for him: not merely the secret of his prayer, but the secret of his apostolate as well, of all his relationships within and outside his Jesuit community, indeed of his relaxation and recreation. As he finished his sharing, I was so deeply touched that I said very spontaneously: "My dear friend, you have discerned your Personal Vocation: the goodness of God!"

This particular incident very specifically allows me now to spell out at different levels the true meaning of "Personal Vocation" - such an intensely rich reality that we cannot take it all in at one glance, as it were. We have to approach it from various angles or at different levels.

1. *Personal Vocation:*
   Secret of Unity and Integration
   at the heart of life

We are all yearning for unity and integration, especially we active apostles. Frankly, the deepest cry of the heart I hear from active apostles in my ministry of spiritual direction is the cry for unity and integration: "I have so many things to do during the day - this, that and the other - that at the end of the day I am all broken up, scattered, dispersed. How I wish

I could be doing only *one thing* in depth!" Is it not true that the more perfect and mature we become, the more simple we become - a simplicity not of impoverishment, but of concentrated richness in depth?

We could, in fact, be doing *only one thing* in depth - like that middle-aged Jesuit. The secret of his prayer was "the goodness of God", for prayer is not something we give to God (we can give nothing to God!); it is rather the opening of our heart so that God can give himself to us. Now, where does our heart open out most if not at that depth of the core of our being where we are most profoundly touched - where we are most truly ourselves, where each of us is *unique?* The secret of that Jesuit's apostolate, of his relationships, of his relaxation and recreation was also "the goodness of God", for in all of these, as he said, he had nothing to do but be "the good God" to others. The "goodness of God" so filled his heart and entire being that he felt, as the unique challenge of his life, that he had to be the channel of God's goodness for others - as much in his apostolate as in his relationships, his recreation and relaxation. His "personal vocation", the goodness of God, had in fact become for him the secret of unity and integration at the heart of his entire life.

But one may well ask how "the goodness of God" is *unrepeatably unique*. It seems so very general: in fact, if you open the Bible you will find "the goodness of God" written on well-nigh every second page. Let me, first of all, pursue the image: if *I* open the Bible and find the words "goodness of God", I shall certainly see in them two important words, but two important words among many other important words. Not so that middle-aged Jesuit: when in opening the Bible his eyes fell on the phrase "goodness of God", it did not register just as two more important words among other important words; no, they stood out in bold relief, burning and aflame with meaning, because they were for him "spirit and life" (cf. Jn 6,63).

There is, besides, a deep psychological reason for this, which helps us grasp how a phrase like "the goodness of God" can indeed be unrepeatably unique. If we have ever attempted to share a profound personal experience with a very close friend, we know by experience that we reach a point in our sharing when we practically give up and helplessly say: "I'm sorry, I can't quite tell you what I truly experienced: if you don't ask me, I know; if you ask me, I don't know!". For "persona est ineffabilis, persona est incommunicabilis": what is most personal is ineffable, what is most personal is incommunicable. Personal knowledge, or what St. Ignatius repeatedly in the Exercises so admirably calls "interior knowledge", is not conceptual knowledge; it is a knowledge of the heart. We can put into words only what we can put into concepts. This is why in sharing a profound personal experience, we can at best approximate to capturing it in poor inadequate human language. Is it surprising that when it comes to formulating what we have discovered as our God-given uniqueness - that is, our profoundest personal experience - we capture it in inadequate human words which sound exteriorly very general, but which speak to us in fact, at the core of our being, of our deepest and truest "self", of our unrepeatable uniqueness?

My own personal experience in helping people discern and live their "personal vocation" bears this out abundantly, as it does in my own particular case. Here are some real "personal vocations" of some very real people, who have very kindly allowed me to make use of this knowledge whenever I see fit to: "I am with you"; "patient love"; "unconditional acceptance"; "remain in my love"; "simply gift"; "only He always can there" (the operative word in this particular case is "there", which is something most profoundly personal to the one concerned). Indeed, I have not the slightest shadow of doubt that the personal vocation of the God-man Jesus was captured in but one single word - "Abba" - which summed up his entire life and mission; it shouts itself out at me from the gospels (read, for example, Jn 5-10 to catch the only argument Jesus has in his controversy with the scribes and the pharisees; or again Lk 10,21 to see Jesus' reaction in his experience of exultant consolation, and Lk 22,39ff for his reaction in the depths of desolation - it is always "Abba"!). All the personal vocations I have cited above sound very general to us; so does Jesus' "Abba". We too say "Abba", for Jesus has shared his "Abba" with us. But what "Abba" meant to Jesus was something very personal and unique, very different from what the word means to us; of this unrepeatable uniqueness we get a glimpse in the gospels. So the formulation in words of the "personal vocation" sounds very general to those who read it or hear of it. What it says, however, to the particular individual whose "personal vocation" it is, is unrepeatably unique.

It would come as no surprise, therefore, to realise that several people may, all of them, well capture their "personal vocation" in the same inadequate human words - for example, "I am with you". But what these words mean to each of these several people is unique and unrepeatably so - experience has taught me this richly in my ministry of spiritual direction where I get a "feel" of this peculiar uniqueness in the particular person's total reaction to experience and whole bearing in life.

2. *Personal Vocation:*
Unique God-given Meaning in life

About a year and a half after I had been graced
with the discernment of my own "personal vocation", I read for the first time Victor Frankl's "Man's
Search For Meaning". As I read through it, my eyes
kept popping out all the time: I resonated deeply with
all that Frankl shared, and I kept telling myself excit-
edly and repeatedly: "I think I know what this man is
talking about". For in his book Frankl relates how he
came to discover his new school of psychotherapy -
"Logotherapy" - in the Nazi concentration camp of
Auschwitz where he had been interned. He tells
how, with his trained clinical eye, he began to per-
ceive that his fellow prisoners were wasting away
and dying physically because primarily they were
wasting away and dying psychologically: they had
no "meaning" to live for and so they gave up the
struggle and buckled under. Very unobtrusively
Frankl started to pick up "meanings" in the lives of
his fellow prisoners in casual conversation with
them; then, he began very naturally and impercepti-
bly to feed these same "meanings" back into the lives

33

of those respective fellow prisoners. What he noticed in sheer wonder - and he gives several concrete examples of this in his book - was that these companions of his, who had practically surrendered to their fate in the concentration camp, came suddenly alive and could go through any torture, any trial, any hardship in the camp thanks to the "meaning" or "meanings" which had been injected back into their lives and which they had made personally their own. So it was that Frankl discovered and later developed his "Logotherapy" - that is, making people whole (= "therapy") by giving "meaning" (= "logos") to their lives. For the primary signification of "logos" is "meaning"; its secondary signification is "word".

But as I read and reread, practically devoured, Frankl's book I gathered that Frankl spoke of one among many possible man-given "meanings" in a person's life, that he spoke on the level of psychology. What I had been taught by God, I realised, was on the level of spirituality; not one among many possible man-given "meanings", but *the unique God-given meaning* in a person's life. As a student of both psychology and spirituality, I have always held, and been increasingly confirmed in my conviction, that these two disciplines - indeed, these two worlds - must never be divorced one from the other: the two, like nature and grace, are intimately and organically related. It is just my way of putting it when I say: spirituality is the highest or the deepest level of psychology, whichever way one wants to look at it.

Further, there exists a close and intimate link between the two aspects of "personal vocation" I have so far highlighted. The "personal vocation" is, in fact, the secret of unity and integration at the heart of a whole life *precisely* because it is the unique God-given meaning in life. For nothing so unifies and integrates in depth as "meaning"; we spontaneously shed what is meaningless, to remain with and interiorise and assimilate what is meaningful.

A familiar example will make this clear. When we were innocent of psychology, we used to speak of "solving" people's problems. If I might use an image, this was something like taking a pair of scissors, "lopping off" the problem and chucking it away. We no longer speak like this. I know I cannot wish away my real history: what has been a "problem" in my life will always remain part of me. If it is no longer "problematic", it is not because it has ceased to be part of me and my history. It is no longer problematic, we say - and we might note well the language we are currently using - because it has now "fallen into place", because it "makes sense", because it is "filled with meaning", because it has become "integrated". It was problematic when it was sticking out uncomfortably like an edge, as it were; it has now got "rounded off", it is now "integrated" into my life.

3. *Personal Vocation:*
   Christological Perspectives

Objectively speaking, no call comes from God to any person except in the person of Christ Jesus; and no person makes a response to God's call except in the person of Christ Jesus. This is only one way of expressing the fundamental biblical truth of Christ's unique mediation: "There is one God, and there is one mediator between God and men, the man Christ Jesus" (1 Tim 2,5).

So all vocations are in Christ Jesus: the personality of Christ Jesus is so infinitely rich that it embraces all calls and vocations. If then each of us has a "personal vocation", this can only be in Christ Jesus. This means that there is a facet of the personality of Christ Jesus, a "face" of Christ Jesus, which is proper to each one of us, so that each one of us can in very truth speak of "*my* Jesus" - not just "piously", but in a deep theological and doctrinal sense.

In fact, this is what the theology of Christian baptism very significantly points to. The New Testament phrase "to be baptised into Christ Jesus" (= *baptizein eis Christon Iêsoun*- e.g., Rom 6,3; Gal 3,27) suggests that each of us has been "plunged into" (=*baptizein*) Christ Jesus - in mystery, of course. So each of us initially "puts on" or is "clothed in" Christ Jesus in a uniquely personal way. The Father, who cannot be pleased with anyone except with his Son Jesus, discerns the "face" of Jesus in each of us and says: "You are my beloved child; in you I find my delight" (cf. Mk 1,11). The rest of our Christian lives - the Christian endeavour, so to speak - is for each of us to "put on" this uniquely personal Jesus to the stature of maturity. For God's plan for each of us is that we "be conformed to the image of his Son" (Rom 8,29), that "we all attain... to mature manhood, to the measure of the stature of the fulness of Christ" (Eph 4,13) - not just in some generic way, but in a deeply personal and unique way for each of us.

The personal vocation then, it is important to grasp, is not just some abstract personal ideal. No, it is a *person* - the person of Christ Jesus himself in a deeply unique way. For me, then, I can in very truth speak of "*my* Jesus", thus transforming my whole Christian life into what I was always taught it to be but never shown how: in very truth, a maturing, profoundly interpersonal love relationship between Christ Jesus and me - one opening out, surely, onto my social responsibilities and commitments in Christian witness and mission.

To return to my story of the middle-aged Jesuit, who discerned his personal vocation to be "the goodness of God": who was *his* Christ Jesus? Why, the *Good* Jesus, of the parable of the *Good* Samaritan, or of the parable of the *Good* Shepherd, or of the Jesus about whom Acts 10,38 says, succinctly summing up his entire life and mission, "he went about doing *good*".

Now we can begin to appreciate in real depth why the personal vocation is the unique God-given meaning in a person's life. Because for God the Father there is no "meaning" outside Christ Jesus: Christ Jesus is the "logos" of the Father - and "logos", we have said, has for its primary signification "meaning". In a marvellous hymn of cosmic sweeping dimensions, St. Paul proclaims that everything has been created in, through and for Christ Jesus; that everything has been recreated, renewed and reconciled in, through and for Christ Jesus (Col 1,12-20). Christ Jesus is the Alpha and the Omega of all creation and of all re-creation; he is the only "meaning" there is for the Father.

And so, the three approaches I have taken to understand the beauty and depth of "personal vocation" are intimately related and bound up together. Indeed, we have seen that the "personal vocation" is the deepest secret of unity and integration at the heart of life precisely because it is the unique God-

given meaning in life; and again, it is the unique God-given meaning in life precisely because it is for each of us his/her personal Jesus. For the Father there is just no meaning outside Christ Jesus.

4. *Consequences for the understanding of Personal Vocation*

From all that has so far been said, it is manifest that the "personal vocation" is not on the same level as the other hierarchically structured vocations. If I were to take a group of ten Jesuit priests, each of them would have the following four levels of hierarchically structured vocation: the Christian, the priestly, the religious and the Jesuit vocations. Now the "personal vocation" of each of them would not be yet another fifth level of hierarchically structured vocation. No: it is rather *the spirit* that animates every one of the four mentioned levels of hierarchically structured vocation. In other words, each of these ten Jesuit priests has *his own personal unique way* of being Christian, priest, religious and Jesuit. And if we grasp what the New Testament so consistently and powerfully teaches on the distinctive note and character of being "Christian" - that is, the typically "Christian" criterion of discernment which is self-gift and self-surrender or, as we commonly call it, "the cross" in its theological and spiritual sense - then every single one of us has, in his/her "personal vocation", his/her own unique way of giving and surrendering self in any human experience. The implications of this for a profound personal transformation in life cannot be lost on any of us. I shall return to them in the last chapter of this little book.

Again, it should be abundantly clear that the "personal vocation" is *not* on the level of doing or of function, but on the *level of being*. It is tragic - even literally so - that so many people interpret "vocation" in terms of mere function or of mere doing. Now the level of function or of doing is bound to enter into crisis some day - that is of the very nature of function or of doing. If then, while in crisis, I have no resources of "being" to fall back upon, because my entire understanding of "vocation" is resolved in terms of sheer function and mere doing, I shall be in total *crisis*. This is unfortunately the not infrequent tragic story of quite a few lives. But if in such a crisis I can fall back on my resources of "being" - so uniquely gifted to me in my "personal vocation" - I need have no fear; I can tide over that crisis, indeed "integrate" it, thanks to the very personal "meaning" on the level of "being" I can find in that very crisis. For all doing flows from being.

It would not be out of place to hint here at the far-reaching consequences of what I have just spelt out for apostolic spirituality. It is no secret that "availability for mission" is one of the distinctive marks of a genuine apostolic spirituality. If my "meaning" in life does indeed lie on the level of "being", far deeper and more radical than on the plane of "doing" where I function, then I can find profound "meaning" in anything that is entrusted to me as "mission". This does not mean that I shall not dialogue with legitimate authority about my gifts, my capabilities, my own experience, even my foibles of character and temperament; but in the last analysis, given such trustful dialogue, I shall be truly "available for mission" according to the pressing needs of the field and of greater apostolic service.

III

THE DISCERNMENT AND
CONFIRMATION OF
PERSONAL VOCATION

1. *Discernment*

Experience has taught me that the *privileged* way of discerning "personal vocation" is through the actual making of the Ignatian Spiritual Exercises. For, as I have shown in the first chapter of this book, the deepest and most radical understanding of the Ignatian "Election" - that is, of the avowed goal of the Exercises - is the discernment of the "personal vocation".

To anyone who has a grasp of the dynamics of the Exercises it is plain that in them the exercitant commits himself/herself to a profound and prolonged praying experience leading to a discerning experience through regular and competent spiritual direction. But this is no haphazard praying experience: its object is the normative process of salvation history. For anyone who wishes to be saved must enter in his/her own unique way into this objective process of salvation history, that is, into the historical development of the mystery of Jesus Christ, the unique mediator and Saviour. Through such a praying experience God frees the person of the exercitant at a progressively deeper level: not only on the obvious plane of sin, imperfection and disorder (First Week), but more profoundly on the level of the exercitant's values and value systems and criteria of living (Second Week contemplations), indeed most deeply then on the level of the securities of life very jealously protected and guarded by the exercitant - first in the obscured recesses of the intellect ("Two Standards" meditation), then in the subtle motivations of the will ("Three Classes" meditation), and finally in the hidden folds of the heart ("Three Kinds of Humility" consideration).

Concomitantly with this progressive dynamic of

deepening inner freedom the exercitant has become more and more open to the action of God's Spirit and to the challenges against it by the action of the counter-spirits. In other words, he/she goes through the ups-and-downs of inner spiritual experience, which are carefully and diligently noted. Looking back over this very experience after having been freed at the deepest existential level (what I have called above the level of the "securities" of life) amounts to looking back over it increasingly with God's eyes, no longer with that jaundiced vision with which the exercitant embarked on the experience of the Exercises. Little wonder that the exercitant can, in a sort of panoramic view of his/her chequered inner experience, bring into bold relief the constant elements of God's presence and action through the signs and fruits of the Spirit. And so is traced the *consistent line or orientation of God's call for salvation* in the unrepeatably unique life of the exercitant. To use Ignatius' language, which we have quoted in the first chapter on "Election", this is for the unrepeatably unique exercitant "the will of God in the disposition (namely, the ordering, the arrangement, the orientation) of his/her life for sal-

vation" (*Sp. Exs.* 1). In other words, this is precisely the exercitant's truest and deepest "self", the unique "name" by which God calls him/her - namely, his/her "personal vocation".

Far from surprising: for, if the exercitant has entered in his/her unrepeatably unique way into the normative process of salvation history through a profound and prolonged praying experience, he/she is sure to be led by the Spirit through a process of deepening inner freedom to discover or discern the reflection of that objective, normative line of salvation in his/her unique life - in other words, he/she will discern the "personal vocation". And if we recall that the objective process of salvation history is, in deeply personalistic terms, the historical development of the mystery of the unique Saviour and Mediator Jesus Christ, then what the exercitant eventually ends up discerning is, in very truth, the unique "face" of his/her Jesus.

2. *Confirmation*

Apart from the particular "confirmation" of

"Election" (in our case, the "personal vocation") which takes place, within the dynamics of the Exercises, in what Ignatius calls the Third and Fourth Weeks, my experience of directing retreats has taught me two very special lines of "confirmation" of the personal vocation.

a) Since I have for the last thirty-one years been regularly gearing the experience of the Spiritual Exercises of St. Ignatius to the discernment of "personal vocation" - this will readily be understood in the light of my profoundest conviction about the real, radical meaning of the Ignatian "Election" - I have come to observe certain very consistent features of the retreatant's experience during the period of "confirmation" following the actual discernment of the personal vocation.

With a certain thrill of discovery the retreatant "wakes up" ever more deeply to the fact that the "personal vocation" he/she has discerned has been amazingly present in his/her concrete history from the very beginning. It is quite an experience, in fact, to listen to the retreatant as he/she enthusiastically traces the presence of his/her particular "personal vocation" through the different stages of his/her concrete history. My response to such enthusiastic sharing on the part of the retreatant is always a very quiet comment: "Are you surprised that your personal vocation has been present all through your life history? If this is truly your personal vocation, then it *should* be present: it was not given to you now in this retreat but, to use the Scriptural phrase, 'from your mother's womb' (cf Is 49,1: 'The Lord called me from the womb, from the body of my mother he named my name'). You have just 'awoken' to it now, you have discovered or 'discerned' it now. It was given to you from the beginning".

One very significant line of "confirmation" of one's personal vocation is, therefore, that it is *written into one's concrete history and into the inner dynamism* (that is, the movement of the inner forces) of one's life.

I have hinted above at my conviction, born of concrete experience, about the intimate relationship between psychology and spirituality. I find this extraordinarily confirmed in the fact that so many of the modern schools of psychology and psychological counselling are coming around to what I have just described as a very significant way of confirming one's personal vocation. Transactional Analysis, for instance, is speaking of "life-scripts"; the Journal Workshop of Ira Progoff is training people to discover their "life-lines" through keeping a personal journal; more recently "Psychosynthesis" is gearing people to trace the "synthesis patterns" in their lives. What, I ask after all I have said about the "personal vocation", is more fundamentally and radically a person's "life-script", or a person's "life-line", or for that matter a person's "synthesis pattern" in life, than his/her personal vocation? And, be it noted well, while Transactional Analysis reveals a person's many "life-scripts", and the Progoff Journal Workshop leads to several "life-lines" for a particular individual, and again Psychosynthesis comes up with various "synthesis patterns" in someone's life, the "Personal Vocation" is the *unique* God-given "life-script", or "life-line", or even "synthesis pattern" in life. This bears out once again what I said earlier of my conviction that spirituality is the deepest or highest level of psychology, whichever way one chooses to look at it.

b) A very good question that may well be raised about the "personal vocation" is: will the "personal vocation" always remain the same for a particular person, or will it keep changing as life goes on? The answer to this question reveals a fresh line of confirmation of the personal vocation.

Experience has taught me, as much in my own case as in the case of those I am guiding in the ways of the Spirit, that, while there is something or a certain aspect that never changes - in fact, cannot change - in the personal vocation, there is another thing or another aspect of it which does change with ongoing life. We have already seen that the personal vocation is in its essence a "spirit" that animates all the levels of hierarchically structured vocation: each one, we said, of a group of ten Jesuit priests, for example, has his own unique way or "spirit" of being Christian, priest, religious and Jesuit. This unique way or "spirit" it is that *never changes:* how could it, if it is given me by God as my uniqueness "from my mother's womb" for my entire life-span and history? But, in our present incarnational economy, there is no realm for "pure" spirit: spirit is always incarnate, enfleshed, embodied. It is this incarnation, then, this concrete enfleshment and embodiment which keeps changing with changing life-circumstances. And so one's personal vocation receives a new "aspect", a new "colouring", a new "deepening" as life moves on.

To find the same, and yet not quite the same, in one's personal vocation as life marches on through changing circumstances is, therefore, precisely yet another powerful way of confirming one's personal vocation. This dynamic character of the personal vocation shows how very deeply it is linked with life and life-transformation: it is proper of anything organic and living to keep developing, while at the same time remaining rooted in one and the same fundamental identity.

In the last analysis, we realise, it is peculiarly characteristic of "meaning" that it lasts and perdures. We never get bored with "meaning": in fact, along life's pilgrimage we keep shedding what is "meaningless", but hold on to what is "meaningful". What happens to "meaning" is that it keeps on becoming ever more deeply "meaningful". If such, in general, is the import of "meaning", what shall we say of the radical and unique God-given "meaning" in a person's life that is his/her "personal vocation"?

TRAN   ON IN DEPTH
THROUGH   NAL VOCATION

Though everythin   far been explained
about the "person   has already shed
much light on the pr   nsformation en-
tailed in the discernm   ul living out of
the same, I would now   ght, and dwell
on, some of its particula   consequences
for daily life and ministry

1. Daily decision-making

It is no secret that *discernme*   he in-
word in Christian spirituality today   state
of the world and of the Church re   ing
need and urgency.

When it comes to *discernment for decision-making* - by the way, this is precisely one of St. Ignatius' most original contributions, through his masterly Spiritual Exercises, to the Christian tradition on discernment - it is frequently said, and even written, that the process of discernment is far too time-consuming and complicated to be employed in the details of daily decision-making. For this the best we can do, so they say, is to use a prudential process to reach a decision: a quick weighing-up of the "pros" and the "cons", then deciding for the side that carries the weightier reasons.

I strongly disagree: I am convinced that the "personal vocation", once discerned, becomes *the criterion of discernment* for every decision in life, even for the daily details of decision-making. For my "personal vocation" is for me "God's will" in the deepest theological meaning of this much-repeated and much-misused phrase. If then I am faced with an option between two alternatives, it is my "personal vocation" that will help me decide through *discernment* which alternative is God's call, God's will *for me*. Checking the two alternatives separately over against the attitude of my "personal vocation", which I put on in depth, I can interiorly "experience" in a matter of minutes which alternative "fits in with" my personal vocation and which "jars over against" it. For my personal vocation is the fundamental consolation of my life; putting it on in depth gets me immediately in touch with my personal Jesus. That alternative, then, which strengthens and deepens my fundamental consolation, is the Lord's call to unique and specific me.

In the whole renewal of ethics and moral theology we are speaking much today of an "existential ethic". In other words, in every option with which I am faced, there is a call to *unique me*. If both alternatives in a concrete option to be made are in fact good, I am not morally free to choose either - that would be tantamount to being an Old-Testament person, led by the moral criterion of right and wrong, good and bad. No, for me as a New Testament person, there is a call of "greater love": it is the call of my personal Jesus to unique and specific me. And the criterion for the discernment of this unique and specific call is none other than my "personal vocation". If, after discerning it through my personal vocation, I follow this call, I am living out a profoundly personal love relationship with the Lord. If I choose to neglect and ignore it in practice, I am not just transgressing a moral law - something like breaking a traffic law or regulation; I am, in fact, betraying a personal love. What quality and depth of personal transformation this entails is evident: I need hardly labour the point here.

In this light I have begun to grasp at a new level of depth what St. Ignatius really means by his characteristic "magis", his "greater love" and "greater service, praise and glory of the Divine Majesty". The Ignatian "greater" and "magis" make no reference whatever to a quantitative element or factor: it has to do with the qualitative "uniqueness" or "specificity" of a particular person's response. In other words, it has direct reference to what I have termed the "personal vocation". Again, new light has been shed for me on what Ignatius so insightfully teaches about the primacy of "the interior law of charity and love which the Holy Spirit is wont to write and imprint on the hearts of men" (*Consts.*

134). Is not this the New Testament law which the prophets foretold God would put into our hearts (cf. Jer 31,31-34; Ez 11,17-20; 36,24-28)? And what is this personalised law of "greater love" if not the very reality of the "personal vocation"? How very far-reaching all this is for the tone and quality of Christian life and ministry!

2. *Finding God in all things*

One's personal vocation is one's *unique* way of being "Christian" - namely, as we have shown earlier, one's unique way of giving and surrendering self in *any* human experience. This amounts to saying that no matter what human experience one is going through, one can get in touch with the Lord in one's uniquely personal way in and through that very human experience. In other words, one can find God in all things - or, to use Jerome Nadal's celebrated phrase, one can be "simul in actione contemplativus" (contemplative in one's very action).

Another way of expressing this, which emerges from the profound dynamics of the Exercises, is that one must have a growing inner freedom, a progressively "free heart" in order to find God in all things, to love Him in all creatures and all creatures in Him according to His most holy will (cf. the Contemplation to Attain Love, as the fruit of the process of deepening inner freedom operative right through the Exercises: *Sp. Exs.* 233, cf. also *Consts.* 288). Now the Lord has gifted each one of us with a *personal* secret of becoming and staying "free" in the midst of any and every human experience - precisely each one's "personal vocation".

All this sheds fresh and abundant light on what St. Ignatius popularised through his Exercises in the form of some very concrete and specific means to achieve "inner freedom" at the heart of real life - namely, the Examination of Conscience and the Particular Examen.

Rightly understood, the Examination of Conscience is not an exercise of mere morality: it is the daily exercise of *discernment.* It is the typical New

Testament exercise in which I seek to be an authentic Christian in and through my real daily experience. For it is only once I have *consciously accepted* my real concrete experience, whatever it be, that I can take up a *Christian attitude* with respect to it - that is, give and surrender myself to the Lord, or become "free" for Him, in and through that very real experience. And I always have my own *unique way* and *personal secret* of doing precisely this, thanks to my "personal vocation". Little wonder that we have rechristened this typically Christian exercise of discernment as the "Consciousness Examen". Here then is our renewed understanding of it today: it is, in prayer, a reorientation of the heart which begins in thanksgiving, then moves towards being centred on the Lord through one's very real experience consciously accepted. That there is a *uniquely personal* way of doing precisely this is the profound and far-reaching significance of "personal vocation" for daily discernment[1].

And what is the "Particular Examen"? Not until

1   For a fuller understanding of the "Consciousness Examen", see below: APPENDIX I.

I had been gifted with the transforming grace of my own personal vocation and experienced its power in daily life and ministry, did I grasp the authentic meaning of the "Particular Examen", and how it could literally be what the classical spiritual authors termed it, namely, "the pulse of the spiritual life". A person's "particular examen", I have come to realise deeply, is the examen which is *particular,* or *specific,* or *unique* to that particular person. No different, therefore, from that particular individual's "personal vocation"!! And so it is a person's unique criterion of Christian discernment in the maelstrom of human experience, that person's unique and specific way of disposing himself/herself to encounter the Lord in any and every human situation. In the last analysis, it is one's uniquely personal way of "finding God in all things". Would it then be too outlandish to infer that living one's "particular examen" is actually the whole sweep of one's spiritual life? For, only if I am living *God-given meaning* at the heart of my life, am I truly alive; else, I am as good as dead. Is this not what we call "pulse"?![2]

2   For a fuller understanding of the "Particular Examen", see below: APPENDIX II.

3. *Formation: basic and ongoing*

In the field of formation or education or pedago-gy, it is axiomatic today to affirm that what radical-ly forms or educates a person is not "input" from the outside, but the releasing or liberating or draw-ing out of the rich inner resources that reside within that person. Modern psychology, especially educa-tional psychology, has established this beyond doubt. The very etymological roots of the word "ed-ucate" (Latin *educere*) suggest this process of "draw-ing out" the riches and resources that lie within.

Now what are the richest resources that reside within a person if not his/her unrepeatable unique-ness and truest "self"? To help a person discover or discern these inmost resources of "personal voca-tion" is then radically and fundamentally to form or educate him/her in the deepest sense. All other "in-put" from without will in effect be truly formative to the extent it can relate to this uniquely personal "meaning"in a particular individual's life. If it does not so relate, it will be shed along the wayside, to be "trodden under foot, for the birds of the air to devour it" (cf. Lk 8,5).

This itself lays bare the true meaning of what we in our days have got accustomed to call "ongoing formation". The heart of ongoing formation does not lie in a "recyclage" programme, valuable as this may be. It is a person's inmost resources of being, that person's unrepeatable "meaning" in life that is the source and secret of all his/her "ongoing formation": that individual's "personal vocation" constitutes his/her live antennae, which are constantly picking up from the atmosphere or the whole range of his/her human experience that which is "meaningful" for his/her growth and ongoing formation. For all "motivation" flows from "meaning". What in the ambience of his/her experience bears no relation to "meaning" in life is left alone; only what does in fact relate to it gets clustered around this personal meaning for ongoing development and growth. One therefore who is living one's personal vocation is a person in constant ongoing formation, in the deepest sense of the word.

CONCLUSION

I must in conclusion confess that I have read nothing, heard nothing to date on "personal vocation": I just have not found anything in writing on the subject - it may well exist, but I acknowledge I am not aware of it; I have heard no one speak of it in any forum. What I have shared above is, in all its details, my lived experience and - I may add - the wondrously rich lived experience of many persons whom I have had the grace and the privilege of accompanying in my ministry of the Spirit. What I have shared, therefore, carries no other guarantee but that of deeply lived experience - always, however, theologically backed up.

Not unaware that the charge of exaggerated individualism and of the neglect of social commitment and responsibilities may well be levelled against all I have said on the subject of "Personal

Vocation", I have a final word to confide - this, too, stems not from theory, but from lived experience.

There is a world of difference between "individualism" and "personalism". A "person" necessarily connotes a freedom that is open to others, not a being closed in on itself (this latter is "individualism") - one that grows, develops, matures precisely by the interpersonal relationships it establishes. What Carl Rogers has to teach in his "On Becoming A Person" is profoundly insightful: we become more and more deeply "persons" precisely through the interpersonal relationships we establish. "Person" and "community" are not mutually exclusive terms: they are intimately correlative. A "person" becomes a "person" only within community; and a community is a true community only if it is made up of living responsible persons (where the members are making the community tasks and the community goals responsibly their own).

In this context, we shall do well to recall that the "personal vocation" is precisely a person's unrepeatably unique way of *giving and surrendering self* - not of closing in on self. In other words, the "personal vocation" is precisely a person's unrepeatably unique way of opening out onto community - opening out onto social reality, social responsibilities, social commitment.

Very recently I happened in T.S. Eliot's "Old Possum's Book of Practical Cats" on his charming poem "The Naming of Cats". I was so thoroughly excited on reading it, and felt so strongly that it was not just "for children" (as he intended it when he wrote it in the thirties) but very much for adults, that today I regularly close all my sharing on "personal vocation" around the world with this poem. I shall close this little book similarly, with grateful acknowledgement to T.S. Eliot.

THE NAMING OF CATS*

The Naming of Cats is a difficult matter,

It isn't just one of your holiday games;

You may think at first I'm as mad as a hatter

When I tell you, a cat must have THREE DIFFERENT NAMES.

First of all, there's the name that the family use daily,

Such as Peter, Augustus, Alonzo or James,

Such as Victor or Jonathan, George or Bill Bailey —

All of them sensible everyday names.

There are fancier names if you think they sound sweeter,

Some for the gentlemen, some for the dames:

Such as Plato, Admetus, Electra, Demeter —

But all of them sensible everyday names.

---

* Reprinted here by permission of "Faber and Faber Ltd." from OLD POSSUM'S BOOK OF PRACTICAL CATS by T.S. Eiiot.

But I tell you, a cat needs a name that's particular,

A name that's peculiar, and more dignified,

Else how can he keep up his tail perpendicular,

Or spread out his whiskers, or cherish his pride?

Of names of this kind, I can give you a quorum,

Such as Munkustrap, Quaxo or Coricopat,

Such as Bombalurina or else Jellylorum —

Names that never belong to more than one cat.

But above and beyond there's still one name left over,

And that is the name that you never will guess;

The name that no human research can discover —

But THE CAT HIMSELF KNOWS, and will never confess.

When you notice a cat in profound meditation,

The reason, I tell you, is always the same:

His mind is engaged in a rapt contemplation

Of the thought, of the thought, of the thought of his name:

His ineffable, effable,

Effanineffable

Deep and inscrutable singular Name.

THE CONSCIOUSNESS EXAMEN

For some years now I have been listening to priests and religious and committed laypeople tell me, in retreats and outside them, that they have long given up the practice of the "Examination of Conscience". It has become sheer meaningless routine to them. What, they ask, is the meaning of day after day - sometimes twice a day - going through the same old rigmarole which they were taught to be the "Examination of Conscience": first thanking God for the gifts of creation, redemption, sanctification, vocation, personal gifts, etc., then asking for light to see their sins and faults, then examining themselves to find some sins, etc. (often they can find none, they say, but they must surely have some...), then making an act of contrition and a purpose of amendment - not quite knowing what exactly they are promising to amend, to do or not to do again...

I have been so struck by this repeated story that I have sat back to ask myself why this traditional, yet profound, spiritual exercise has become "routine" for so many committed and consecrated Christians. I think I have come up with an answer: we have made of the "examination of conscience" an exercise of mere *morality;* it is, in fact, the daily exercise of *discernment.*

Morality, as such, belongs to the Old Testament; what is typical of the New Testament is not mere morality, but discernment. As Christians, disciples of Jesus Christ, our criterion of behaviour and action is not merely what is right as opposed to what is wrong, what is good as opposed to what is bad. The New Testament law is that of love, written not on tablets of stone outside of ourselves, but in our hearts within us. The Christian, as New Testament person, asks where is "greater love"; he/she is not morally free to choose either of two alternatives when both are good. The Christian decides through discernment, in seeking to find out where "greater love" beckons him/her. In this sense, as an exercise of discernment, the "Examination of Conscience" is the *typical New Testament exercise.*

Now what is distinctive of Christian discernment is that it is based on *experience:* for the *discernment of spirits* is a sort of sifting through of *interior spiritual experiences* in order to trace their orientation and so determine their origin - if from God, to embrace and make them our own; if from the counter spirit, to reject them. Further, we deal with experience by first becoming *conscious* of our experience; hence, precisely because it is an exercise of discernment, the "Examination of Conscience" is an *examen of consciousness* - consciousness of our real concrete experience, whatever it be.

It is striking that in all the Latin languages the same word is used for both "conscience" and "consciousness": in Latin itself *conscientia* stands for both "conscience" and "consciousness"; in Spanish the same is true of the word *conciencia;* in Italian, again, with the word *coscienza*; and in French, with the word *conscience*. It is Ignatius who through his Spiritual Exercises popularised the *examen de conciencia* - in truth, therefore, the "Consciousness Examen", as an exercise of discernment.

How then, in fact, are we to do this exercise of discernment? What are its specific steps?

1. *Thanksgiving*

Because we are doing a typically *Christian* exercise, we begin with "thanksgiving". The image of the Christian spiritual life is not that of man or woman struggling his/her way up to God. According to the biblical revelation, the primacy or the initiative belongs to God: it is He who is always coming into our lives with His gifts, His grace, His love and power; for us, it is to be *actively receptive* to Him and His saving action.

So, to place our "Consciousness Examen" in its proper context as a *specifically Christian exercise,* we begin by acknowledging God's coming into our lives, His gifts, His grace, His action in us: we *thank* Him.

2. *Experience*

Within the above-mentioned typically Christian context we start our exercise of discernment. This means that we first pick up our real *experience* of the day or half-day, whatever be that experience, positive or negative. If we are to deal with this experience, we can do so only by becoming *conscious* of it, then *accepting* it for what it is.

a) *Consciousness* or *Awareness* of the real experience which has taken place.

b) *Acceptance* of the same

We need to dwell on this particular step of acceptance, because it is too often taken for granted. We would do well to distinguish clearly between "approval" and "acceptance": "approval" or "disapproval" is a *judgement,* "acceptance" or "non-acceptance" is an *attitude.* God cannot "approve" of so many things I say and do, yet in the very same things He "accepts" me *unconditionally* - of this I am absolutely sure and certain. What God does for me, I need to do for myself. Experience has taught me that we either mix up "approval" and "acceptance", "disapproval" and "non-acceptance", or take it for granted that "consciousness" or "awareness" of an experience automatically involves its "acceptance". The fact is that we have a kind of spontaneous inner dynamic of "non-acceptance" operative within each one of us. And one of the great fruits of the experience of the ministry of counselling and spiritual direction is the realisation that "non-acceptance" of real human experience is a fundamental obstacle that in so many good-willed and well-intentioned people is blocking effective human and spiritual growth.

It is worthwhile, perhaps, noting concretely how very spontaneously the inner dynamic of "non-acceptance" tends to take over within us. We either run away from our experience, or get afraid of it, or get guilty about it, or repress and suppress it - all various forms of "non-acceptance". How, I ask, do we *deal with* experience by first making a *tabula rasa* of it?!

Let me take, for example, my awareness or consciousness of having been impatient, having lost my temper and flown off the handle. Very spontaneously, within me, I immediately adopt one of two stances, most often not formulated in words (that's the insidious part of it, for if I captured it in words I would often recognise it for what it is): either I begin to wallow in self-pity, which might sound something like this if it were put into words: "I'm really a good boy, but they don't understand me poor me!"; or I entrench myself in self-justification, which for its part might sound something like this if it were couched in words: "They provoked me, they jolly well got what they deserved!". It is not hard to see that both this self-pity and this self-justification are, in psychological terms, just "non-acceptance".

Or, to show that in my "Consciousness Examen" I am to deal not just with "negative" experiences but with "positive" ones as well, let me take an example of my awareness or consciousness of having been truly serviceable, having generously reached out to others in need. Here, too, I very spontaneously adopt one of two extreme stances: either I begin to "feel bad about feeling good" in the sense that I don't dare acknowledge I have done good (I have been so perfectly trained not to acknowledge the good that I do for fear of being proud and arrogant!); or I so bloat my experience out of proportion that I see myself as the "paragon of all virtue" for having been so serviceable to others (I am ready to be set up and proposed as a model of virtue to others!) - again both subtle forms of "non-acceptance".

This only underlines the absolute need to expend time and effort on truly *accepting* our real experience; we cannot take this "acceptance" for granted.

3. *"Freedom" through Discernment*

Only once we have *consciously accepted* our real concrete experience, whatever it be, can we be genuine *Christians* in and through that same experience. To be distinctively "Christian", we have seen, is to *give and surrender self* to the Lord - that is, to become "free" for the Lord, to open out to the Lord - and, in Him, to others in real and concrete human experience.

Now every single one of us has, in his/her "personal vocation", the *deeply unique personal way* of being "Christian" - that is, of giving and surrendering self, or becoming "free", in any human experience. In other words, every single one of us has a *unique secret and criterion of discernment* in the midst of all our human experience.

So the specific "Christian" step of the "Consciousness Examen" is for us, at this stage, to put on in depth the attitude of our "personal vocation", which will "free" us from ourselves to touch the Lord in and through our real concrete experience. And this, as much in our so-called "negative" as in our "positive" experiences.

Putting all these steps together, I may now offer the following definition or description of the "Consciousness Examen": it is, *in prayer,* a *reorientation of the heart* which begins in thanksgiving, then moves towards being centred on the Lord through one's very real experience consciously accepted.

The Sacrament of Reconciliation is intimately connected with the "Consciousness Examen" as explained above. To most Catholics, who have a true Christian understanding of the sacramental economy, the practice of "confession" as obligatory in the case of serious sin presents, as such, no difficulty. What many of them do not understand and appreciate is the meaning of "devotional confession".

If the "Consciousness Examen" is, as I have said above, my daily effort at giving and surrendering self in the crucible of my real concrete experience - that is, my daily effort at being genuinely "Christian" - then "devotional confession" means bringing, from time to time or at regular intervals (fortnightly, monthly,...), to a peak of sacramental expression this same daily effort at being truly "Christian".

This is best done by concentrating on one or other area, in which the daily effort at self-surrender and self-gift is, through the faithful practice of the "consciousness examen", perceived to be particularly needed. In this way Christian sorrow is concentrated on that specific area, and the grace of the sacrament is also concretely directed towards it for ongoing growth in that precise area of Christian living and ministry. Experience has shown that, in practice, "devotional confession" has often remained ineffective and unproductive in terms of concrete Christian living because of a dispersal of consciousness and effort over many areas and much ground.

THE PARTICULAR EXAMEN

Any talk of the "Particular Examen" immediately conjures up images of generally fruitless efforts made in the early stages of spiritual training at a sort of "spiritual accountancy": either, picking on a faulty or deficient point, totting up day after day one's failures in this regard, and making a determined effort to progressively decrease these failures; or, concentrating on a positive area like a virtue, keeping daily count of the actual practice of that virtue, and making a bid to steadily increase the 'acts' or exercise of that same virtue.

Frankly, if we are to consult the actual experience of so many people who were formed in this practice of the "Particular Examen", we shall have to acknowledge that this kind of exercise of "spiritual accountancy" just did not work: it was abandoned quite early on as "hopeless", as "impossible to keep". No less a person than the great spiritual writer, Father Luis de La Palma - noted Jesuit spiritual director of the late 16th and early 17th century - suggested that in his own expenence and in the experience of those he was guiding this mode of the practice of the "Particular Examen" was by and large fruitless.[1]

And yet, the classical spiritual authors have termed the particular examen "the pulse of the spiritual life"! I recall being told rather authoritatively, when I was a Jesuit novice - though I haven't yet been able to find it documented anywhere - that St. Ignatius admitted he kept his "particular examen" for the last twenty to twenty-five years of his life on vanity, ambition, vainglory. Be that as it may, one is inclined to dismiss all talk of the particular examen in terms like "the pulse of the spiritual life" as so much pious exaggeration on the part of spiritual authors. In any case, I myself dismissed it as such in my early years of Jesuit training, as I had also dismissed the very suggestion that St. Ignatius practised his "particular examen" on vanity, ambition, vainglory for

[1]   Cf. his commentary on the Exercises, "Camino Espiritual', in *Obras del P. Luis de la Palma*, pp. 892 ff... esp. 894 (B.A.C., Madrid 1967).

the last twenty to twenty-five years of his life (precisely years when he was experiencing great mystical graces showered on him by God!) - "these saints have always to say something 'pious' about themselves", was my reaction, I recall!

Who, in fact, was this Ignatius of Loyola when God got hold of him on the battle-field of Pamplona by shattering his leg with a canon-ball? He himself tells us in the opening lines of his *Autobiography* (nn. l; 4-6): his only dreams were about worldly honour and worldly glory, about the heroic feats he would perform for his king and for his lady fair! It was then that God took hold of him and, as I love to say, turned him around 180 degrees! He said to Ignatius: "You are dreaming of your greatest glory; do you know the *meaning* I have given to your life? Not your greatest glory, but my greatest glory *(la mayor gloria de Dios)*!" I have no doubt that the "personal vocation" of Ignatius of Loyola was *la mayor gloria de Dios* - the greater or the greatest possible glory of God. Ignatius never forgot this all his life long; indeed, the greater the gifts that God would shower on him, the more vigilant would he be to make sure that he would not turn it to his greatest possible glory (he had a penchant for this, he knew only too well), but to the greatest possible glory of God. Would it then be surprising, should we be able to document it, that Ignatius kept his "particular examen" for the last twenty to twenty-five years of his life on vanity, ambition, vainglory?

What this, but above all my own personal experience together with my ministry of the Spirit, has revealed to me is that the "particular examen" is in truth the examen which is "particular" or "specific" or "unique" to a concrete individual person. What, indeed, is more "particular" or "specific" or "unique" to a given concrete person than his/her "personal vocation"? It is not without significance that the word "particular" in Spanish - and it is St. Ignatius who popularised the "particular examen" through his Spiritual Exercises - is not just the opposite of the word "general", as it happens to be in the English language. In Spanish the word "particular' is often used to mean a specific person, an unrepeatably unique individual - as, for example, *este particular me lo dijo,* meaning "this fellow, and not another, told me so".

The "particular examen" is, therefore, no different from the "personal vocation". In this deepest sense, there are not many subjects of "particular examen"; there is for each person just *one* - his/her "personal vocation" itself. Little wonder that the "particular examen" becomes a person's unique criterion of Christian discernment in the entire gamut of human experience, that person's unique and specific way of disposing himself/herself to encounter the Lord in any and every human situation. In a word, it is one's uniquely personal way of "finding God in all things", of being "contemplative in action". In this way the practice and living out of one's "particular examen" becomes in very truth the whole sweep of one's spiritual life. Would it then be a "pious exaggeration" to affirm that the "particular examen" is indeed "the pulse of the spiritual life"? For one cannot be said to be authentically alive unless one is living *God-given meaning* at the heart of one's life; else, one is as good as dead.

I have referred above to Father Luis de La Palma and his masterly commentary on the Ignatian Exercises, "Camino Espiritual". I had the joy of reading this spiritual classic when I was a young student of philosophy in Barcelona, Spain (1952-1955). Already then, what this celebrated spiritual director had to say about the practice of the "particular examen" had proved very enlightening and, even more, liberating for me.

Eschewing all methods of what I have termed "spiritual accountancy", La Palma offers a refreshingly new approach to the practice of the "particular examen" - even though his understanding of the "particular examen" has still to do with one's concentrating on a particular area (positive or negative) of one's real daily life. His suggestion looks deceptively simple; actually it carries a profound insight into the nature of Christian spiritual life and its growth.

The practice of the "particular examen", says La

Palma, consists in choosing some very definite moments during the day - moments which one can *be sure of* in one's daily schedule, no matter how few in number they may be - and, at these moments, putting on the attitude of the particular area that has been chosen as the subject of the "particular examen". There is absolutely no totting up either of the numer of times one has failed (in the case of a "negative" area), or of the number of times one has actually practised, or exercised oneself in, something (in the case of a "positive" area); all one needs to check is whether one has been faithful to the definite number of moments chosen for the already mentioned putting-on of the attitude.

Deceptively simple, isn't it? And yet, its deep insight is that human freedom has no other role to play in the spiritual life but actively to *dispose* itself for God - God does the rest. To God belongs the initiative and the primacy of action: it is He who is *always* coming into out lives to save and redeem them ("He comes, comes, ever comes", as our great poet laureate Rabindranath Tagore sang in his *Gitanjali*). If our hearts are "disposed" for Him, we shall experience union with the Lord. Concretely, then, what La Palma suggests is no other than a regular "disposing" of oneself to be or do that which one has chosen as the subject of one's "particular examen". If this is done faithfully at the moments determined as sure for one, there is every likelihood that one will not be taken by surprise or caught off-guard: one *will* in fact be or do that which one has carefully and diligently chosen to be or do.

Thus far La Palma. But, having once been gifted with the privileged grace of not only discerning my own "personal vocation" but experiencing its powerful meaning and thrust for the whole sweep of life and ministry, I have grasped even more radically what the true practice of the "particular examen" is. If, as I have shown, the "particular examen" is no different from the "personal vocation", and if the "personal vocation" is one's unrepeatably unique and specific way of actually *disposing* oneself for the Lord, then the most meaningful practice of the "particular examen" is to put on in depth the attitude of one's "personal vocation" at those concrete moments which one has chosen as absolutely sure for oneself in one's daily schedule. This itself readies and disposes one, as no other means can, to meet the Lord in the persons, events and circumstances of time, place and action that punctuate one's daily round of living. It is, in the last analysis, one's uniquely personal way of "finding God in all things".

Finito di stampare
nel mese di maggio 2002

presso la tipografia
"Giovanni Olivieri" di E. Montefoschi
00187 Roma - Via dell'Archetto, 10,11,12